Contents

2 Introduction/The ´
4 Chester 50 CE
6 Chester 78 CE
8 Chester 150 CE
10 Chester 276 CE
12 The Amphitheatre
14 The Fortress Wall
16 The South-East Angle Tower
28 The Hospital
30 The Twentieth Legion
32 Roman Chester today

Symbols used in this guide

- **1** *Roman site, with visible remains*
- **2** *Roman site, with no visible remains*
- **3** *Recreated Roman site or artefact*
- **1** *Speculative Roman camp (see page 4)*
- *Roman wall, with no visible remains*
- *Post-Roman wall, with visible remains*
- **A** *Museum with Roman artefacts and displays*

Reconstructing the past

The images in this book are based on archaeological data produced by Dr David Mason FSA MCIfA and others. The white ghosted areas in the image above show which buildings featured in this book are unknown, but have been included as there was probably some kind of building located in that area.

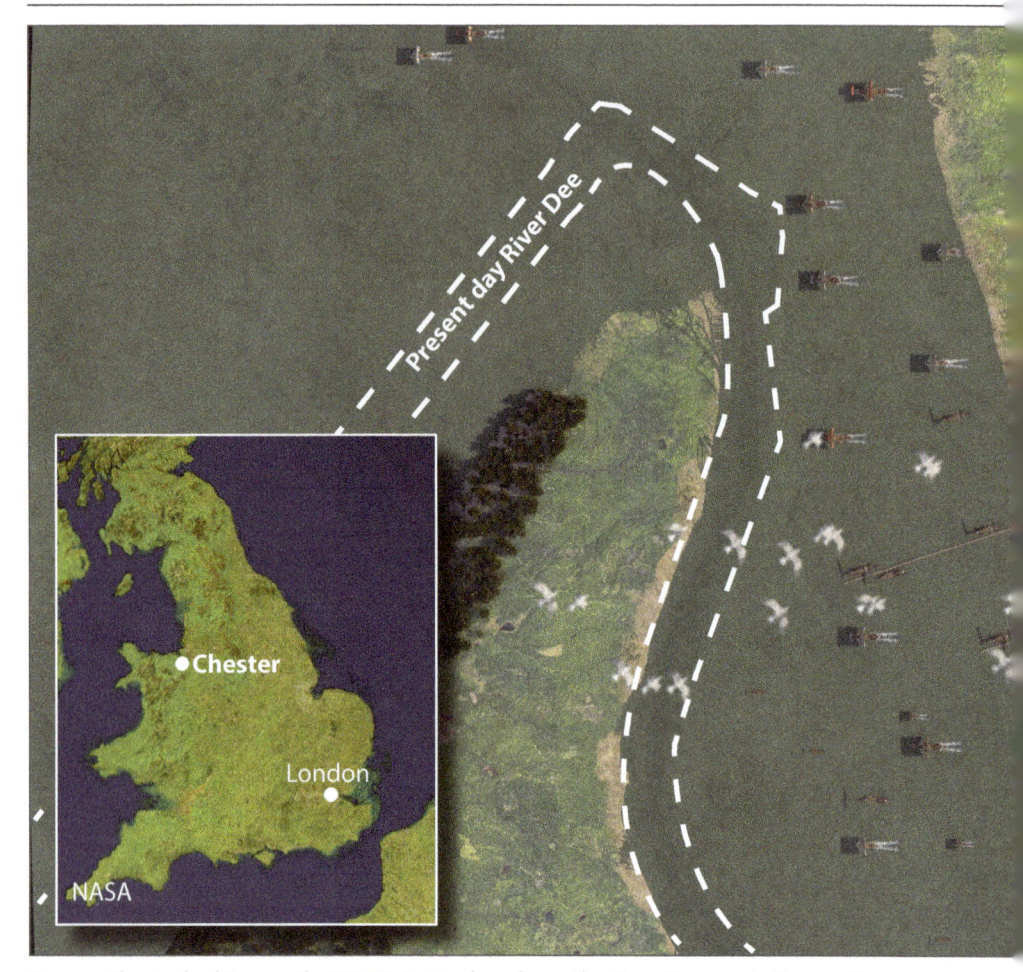

Roman Chester looking north, 276 CE. Notice how large the River Dee was in Roman times.

Introduction

The area where Chester is now located was occupied before the Roman invasion by the *Cornovii*. They were a small tribe who occupied the broad equivalent of the present day Shropshire area. The Romans moved into the area around 50 CE as this allowed them to observe nearby powerful tribes in North Wales and nearby Yorkshire.

The Roman occupation and growth of the city is the focus of this guide, exploring the period from 50 CE to 276 CE. After this date the Roman Empire started a gradual decline and by 410 CE Britain was under constant attack by marauding Anglo-Saxons.

The guide brings to life how Chester **could** have looked, with full-colour images all looking north and detailed maps showing where each site is in present-day Chester.

Towns and cities

The Romans defined towns and cities differently to how we do in the present day. They had three main types of town:
- *A Colonia, which was a rough equivalent of a city.*
- *A Municipium, which was slightly less important than a colonia.*
- *A Civitas capital, which was a broad equivalent of a large market town.*

The Romans called pre-Roman towns 'oppida'.

CGI model based on archaeological data produced by Dr David Mason FSA MCIfA

The Romans

The city of Rome in central Italy was formed around 800 BCE and grew over the centuries into the Roman Empire, which covered most of Europe, the Middle East and North Africa. It was a highly sophisticated and technologically advanced society, with a huge army, major roads and large cities. Britain at that time was a mysterious place with fierce tribes and valuable metals, which became the focus of attempted invasions in 55 BCE and 54 BCE by *Julius Caesar*.

Those invasions were repelled by local tribes and the Romans did not try again to invade Britain for almost 100 years.

By 43 CE the *Emperor Claudius (who needed the army's support)* decided to invade Britain, focusing his initial attack on the east of England.

Around 50 CE Roman forces were moving to occupy the area where Chester now stands...

Visiting Chester

Chester lies about 210 miles north-west of London. There are two main museums which show Roman Chester in depth: the Grosvenor Museum and the Deva Roman Experience. Remains of the Roman city wall and partial remains of other Roman sites, including an amphitheatre can also be seen around the city.

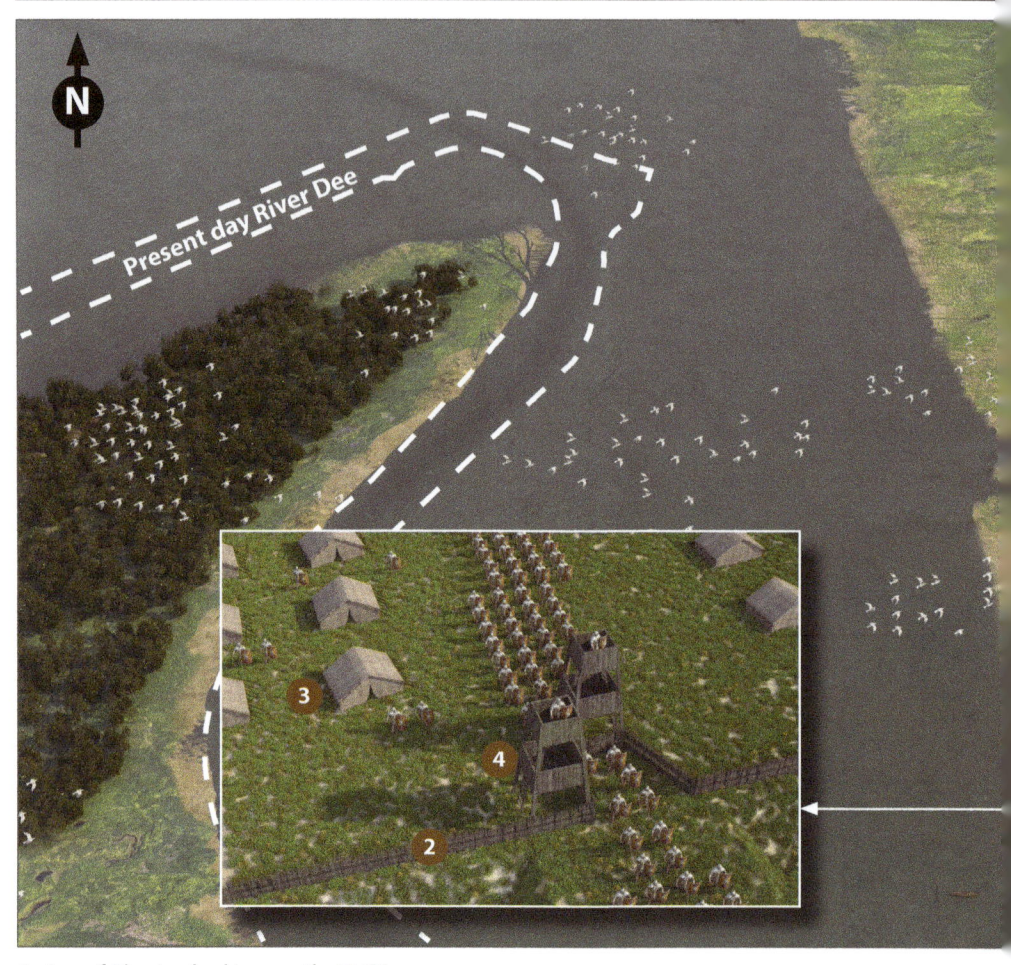

A view of Chester, looking north, 50 CE.

Chester 50 CE

Before the Roman invasion Chester was part of the territory of the *Cornovii*, who occupied the rough equivalent of the Shropshire area. There does not seem to have been a major *Cornovii* settlement in the immediate area, although there were many hill-forts further away. They had settled in the area during the Iron Age and may have been one of the less wealthy tribes. After the invasion of 43 CE, the Romans initially concentrated on the south-east of Britain before slowly moving across the country. Around 50 CE the Romans probably built a temporary *Castra (camp)* where Chester is now located. This would have had tents, ditches and *sudes* (stakes) wall defences, which could be prepared rapidly each night. Nothing was sited too close to the perimeter defences, to stay out of range of enemy thrown weapons such as spears.

Key

- ▪ ▪ *Castra extents*[1]
- ▬ *Future Fortress Walls*
- ❶ *Castra*[1]
- ❷ *Sudes*
- ❸ *Legionary Tent*
- ❹ *Castra entrance*

1. The exact layout of the castra is not known, as it was a temporary structure, but the image and map show how archaeologists believe it could have looked.

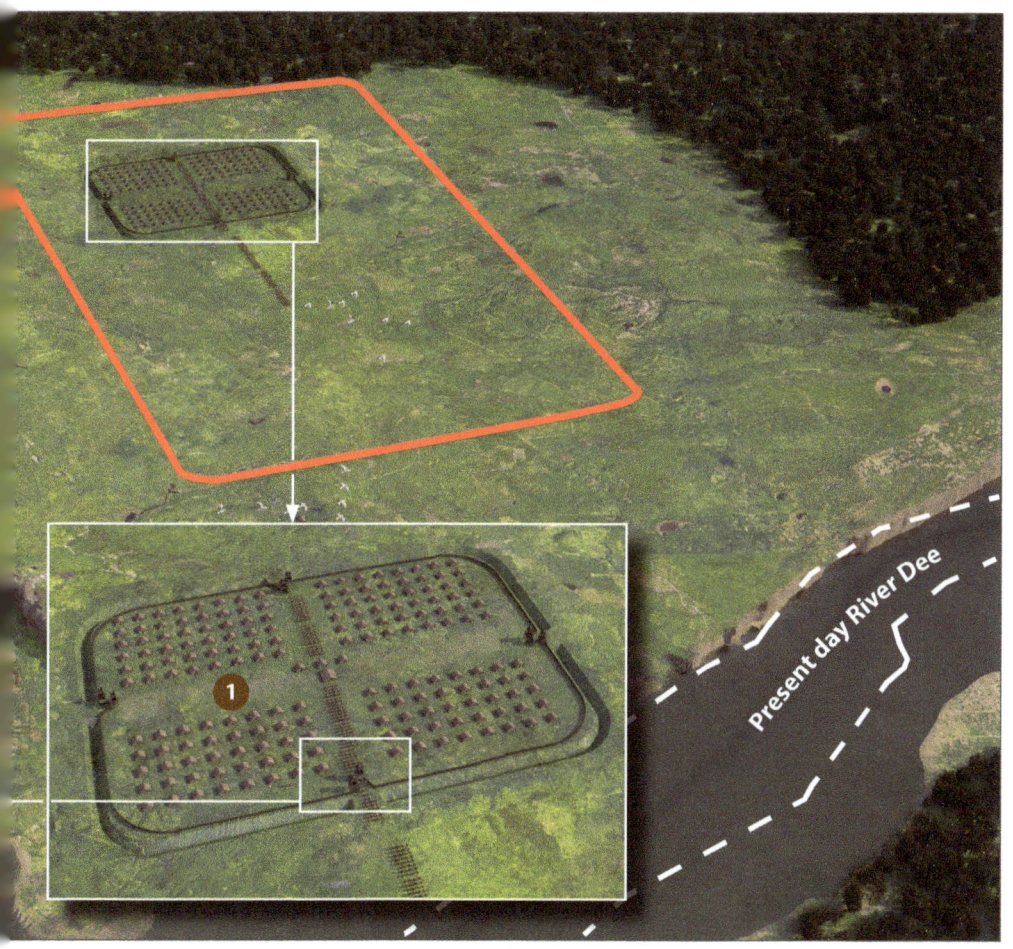

CGI model based on archaeological data produced by Dr David Mason FSA MCIfA

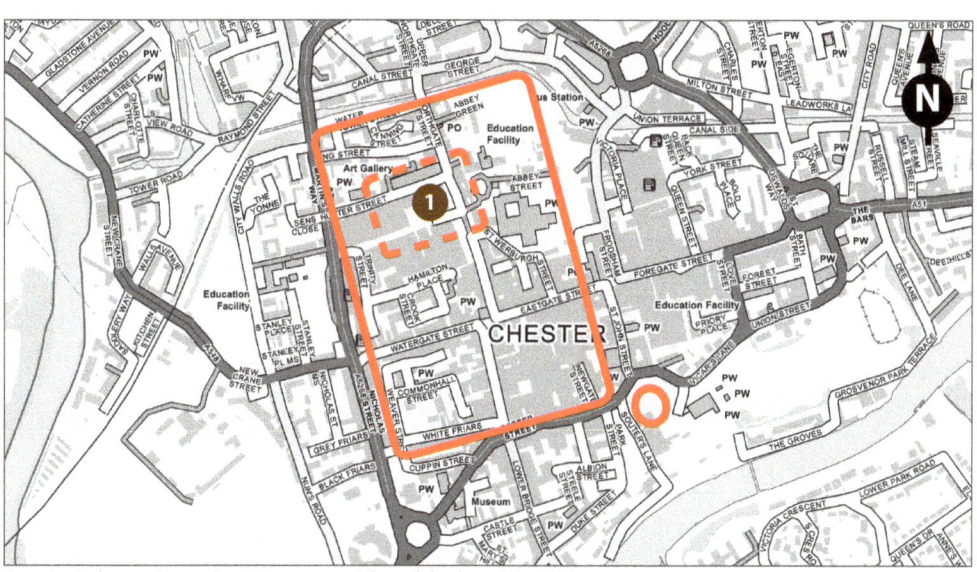

A view of Chester, showing the mostly timber constructed buildings, 78 CE.

Chester 78 CE

Around 76 CE a permanent fortress, named *Deva*[1], was established by the *Legio II Adiutrix, (Second Legion 'Helper')* and would have housed over 5000 men. Around 80 CE the *Legio XX Valeria Victrix (Twentieth Victorious Valeria Legion)* replaced the *Legio II Adiutrix*. It seems that the fortress was located in this area partly to keep the local tribes under control and partly as a possible launch site for an invasion of Ireland[2], which ultimately was abandoned. It also proved an ideal location for transporting lead[3] and silver from Flintshire mines which were close to Chester.

1. Deva was a Roman version of a local word meaning goddess.
2. The Roman historian, Tacitus, said that merchants were consulted about Ireland's geography to aid planning an invasion.
3. The Grosvenor Museum has large lead ingots, which date from the Roman period.

Key

— Roman Walls
1. Roman Fortress
2. Wooden Amphitheatre
3. Barracks
4. Fortress Bathhouse
5. Incomplete foundations of Elliptical Building (see page 18)
6. Fortress Principia (see page 20)
7. Reduced trees compared to 50 CE (see page 4). Large numbers of trees were cut down to build the fortress.

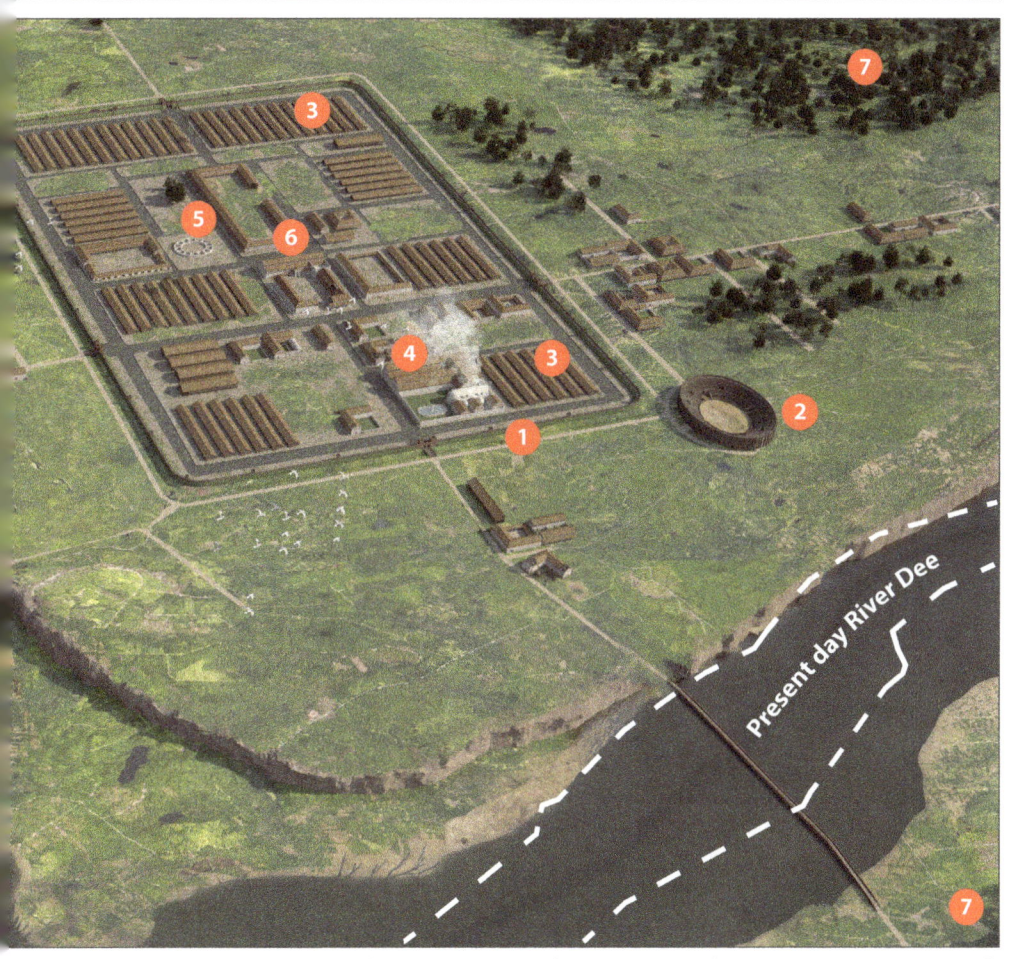

CGI model based on archaeological data produced by Dr David Mason FSA MCIfA

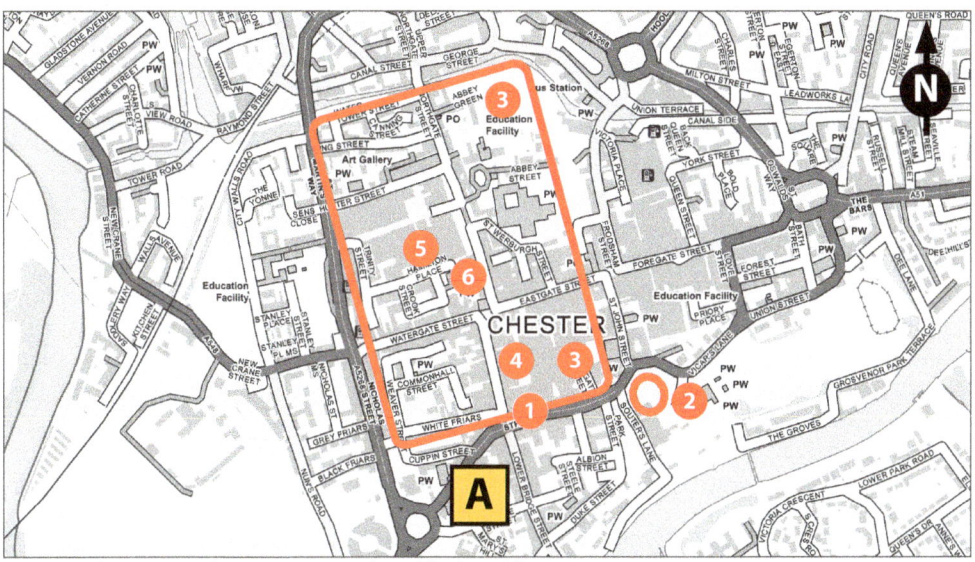

Contains Ordnance Survey data © Crown copyright and database right 2025

A view of Chester, showing the abandoned partially constructed buildings, 150 CE.

Chester 150 CE

Another advantage to locating a fortress in the Chester area was that it was well connected to the major fortresses at Caerleon, York and the growing city of *Londinium (London)*. Initially most of the buildings in the fortress were built from wood, before around 120 CE the fortress[1] was upgraded with stone buildings. Strangely, during the middle of this construction, the fortress was left practically unoccupied for around 40 years while the legion was redeployed to the north. Most of Roman Chester at this time was an abandoned building site, with partially completed buildings. Rather than acting as a fortress it was more like a run-down depot, supplying other fortresses. A shrine to the Roman goddess of wisdom, *Minerva*, was built at this time. This can still be seen in the present day and is just off the map, as shown by the blue arrow.

1. The fortress was later known as Deva Victrix.

Key
— Roman Walls
1. Roman Fortress
2. Possible military storehouses
3. Amphitheatre, possibly used as a rubbish dump

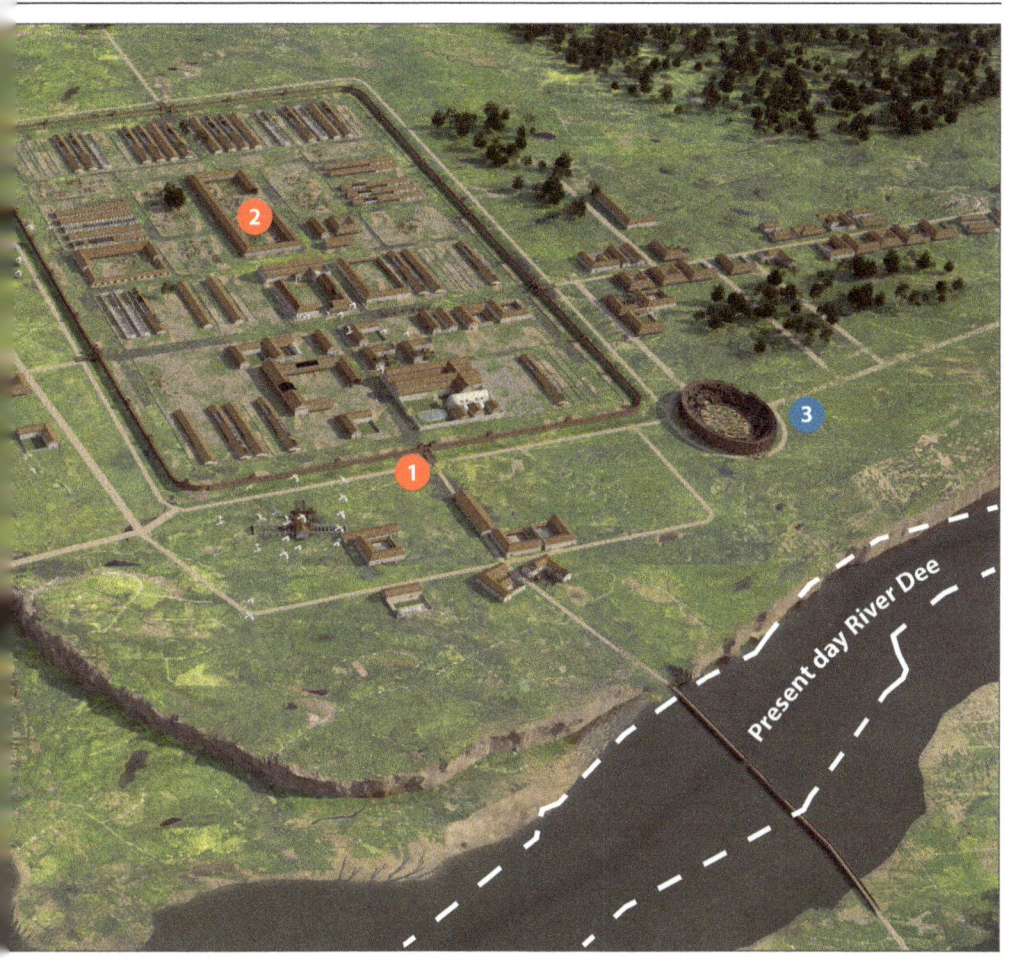

CGI model based on archaeological data produced by Dr David Mason FSA MCIfA

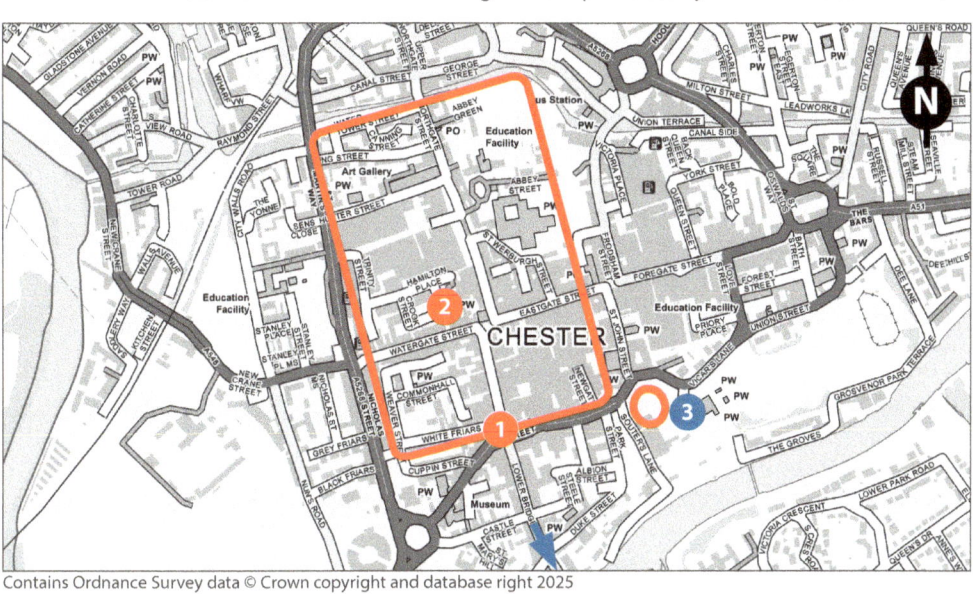

Contains Ordnance Survey data © Crown copyright and database right 2025

A view of Chester, looking north, 276 CE.

Chester 276 CE

Around 230 CE Roman Chester began to be completely overhauled, including the completion of the unusual Elliptical Building *(see page 18)*. It seems that the design of the fortress at Chester was the result of a grand plan which never was seen through. It was much larger than the fortresses at Caerleon and Lincoln. Combined with complex walls and buildings, it may have been intended to be the centre of a combined Britain and Ireland. Although that never happened, many of the original plans were mostly followed when Chester was rebuilt along with the growing *canabe*[1] where traders lived. The main image also shows how much the River Dee has changed since Roman times. It was wider and deeper, allowing a constant flow of ships, and it is thought a large jetty was built to allow ships to be unloaded, whatever the level of the river.

1. *A settlement that grew around a fortress.*

Key

— Roman Wall
1. Road to York, via Northwich
2. Road towards Irish Sea
3. Roman Port *(see page 24)*
4. Road to London, via Whitchurch
5. Bathhouse
6. Roman Wall
7. Principia *(see page 20)*
8. Amphitheatre
9. South-East Angle Tower
10. Mansio[2]

2. *A rest area for travelling officials.*

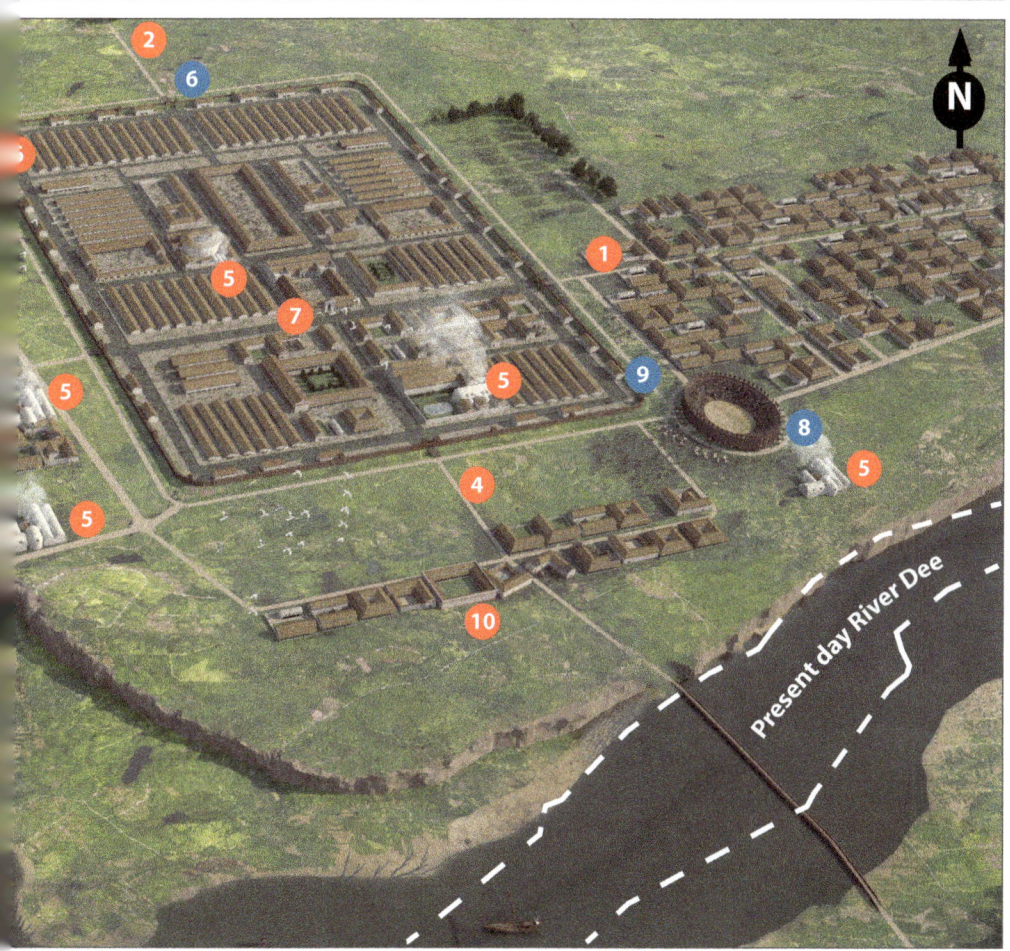

CGI model based on archaeological data produced by Dr David Mason FSA MCIfA

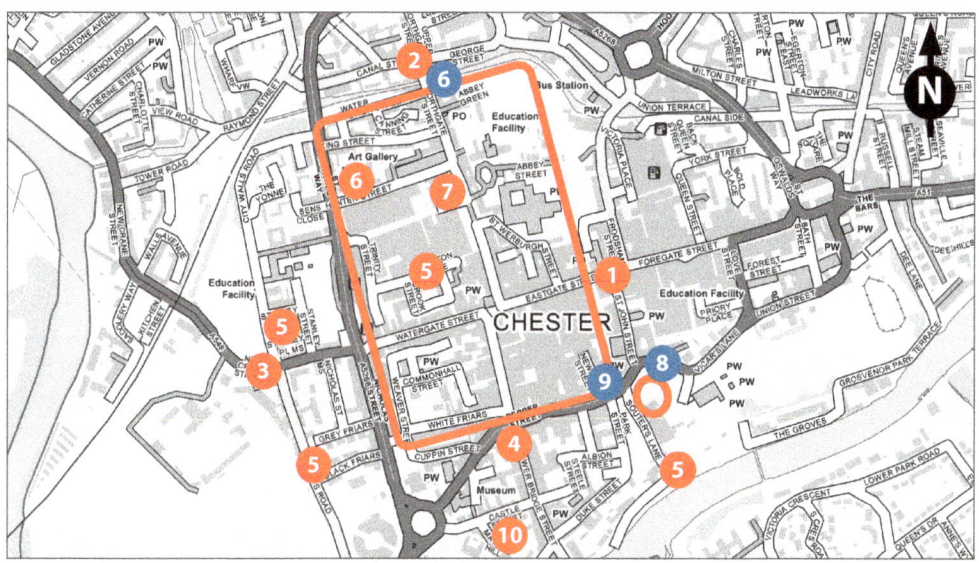

Contains Ordnance Survey data © Crown copyright and database right 2025

12. The Amphitheatre

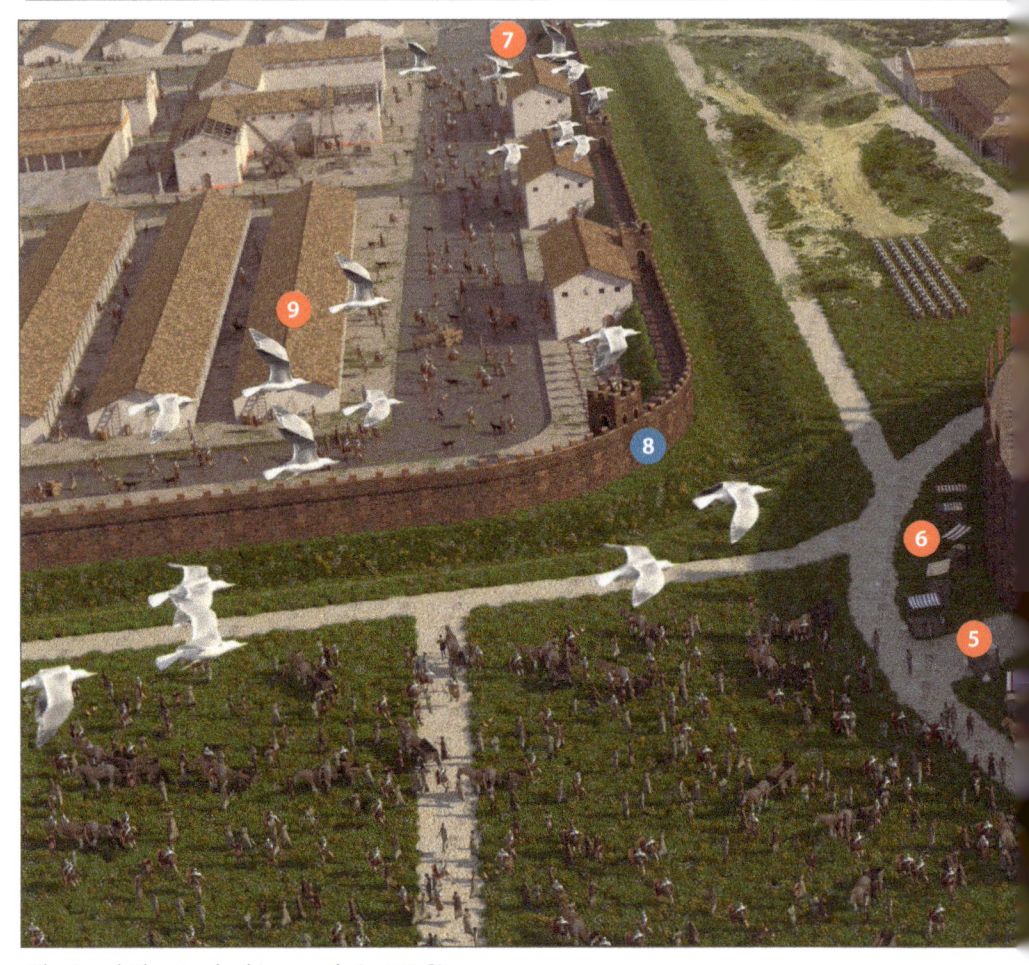

The Amphitheatre, looking north, in 276 CE.

The Amphitheatre

In 1929 builders unearthed the largest Roman amphitheatre found in Britain, yet it almost ended up covered by a bypass road. It was built around 78 CE to provide entertainment for the soldiers based at the fortress. About 100 CE the amphitheatre was rebuilt in stone and also had a shrine[1] dedicated by a centurion to the goddess *Nemesis*.[2] Amphitheatres used by the legions often had military events, some dedicated to the gods. But there would probably also have been gladiators fighting, to entertain the soldiers. The amphitheatre would have been a huge building seating up to 7000 soldiers, and inside the central arena would be covered in sand to stop the gladiators slipping during combat. The amphitheatre was later abandoned, becoming a rubbish dump before it was repaired in 275 CE.

1. It was built for the gladiators to pray before the 'games'.
2. Nemesis was the goddess of retribution (Destiny).

Key

— Roman Walls
1. Amphitheatre
2. Shrine to Nemesis
3. Arena
4. Cavea (seating area)
5. Vomitorium (exit)
6. Market stall
7. Eastgate
8. South-east Angle Tower
9. Barracks

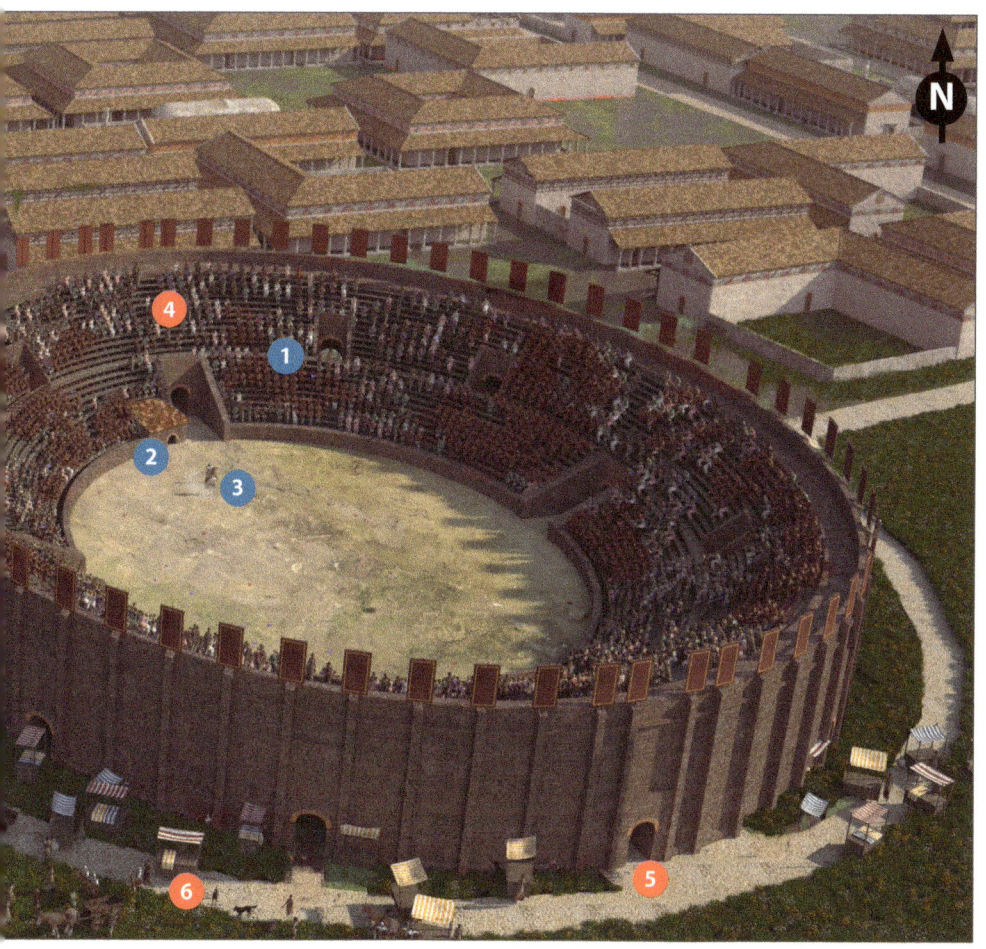

CGI model based on archaeological data produced by Dr David Mason FSA MCIfA

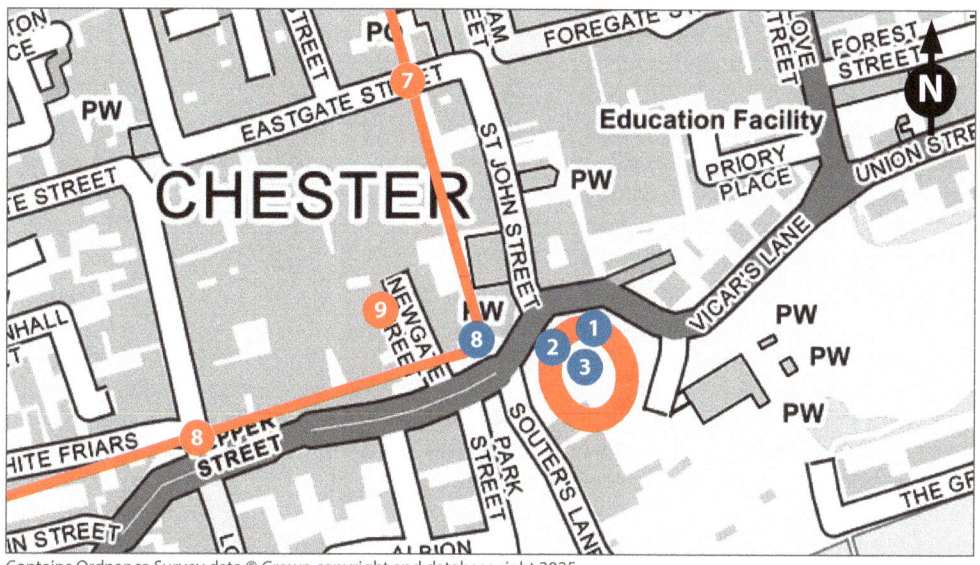

Contains Ordnance Survey data © Crown copyright and database right 2025

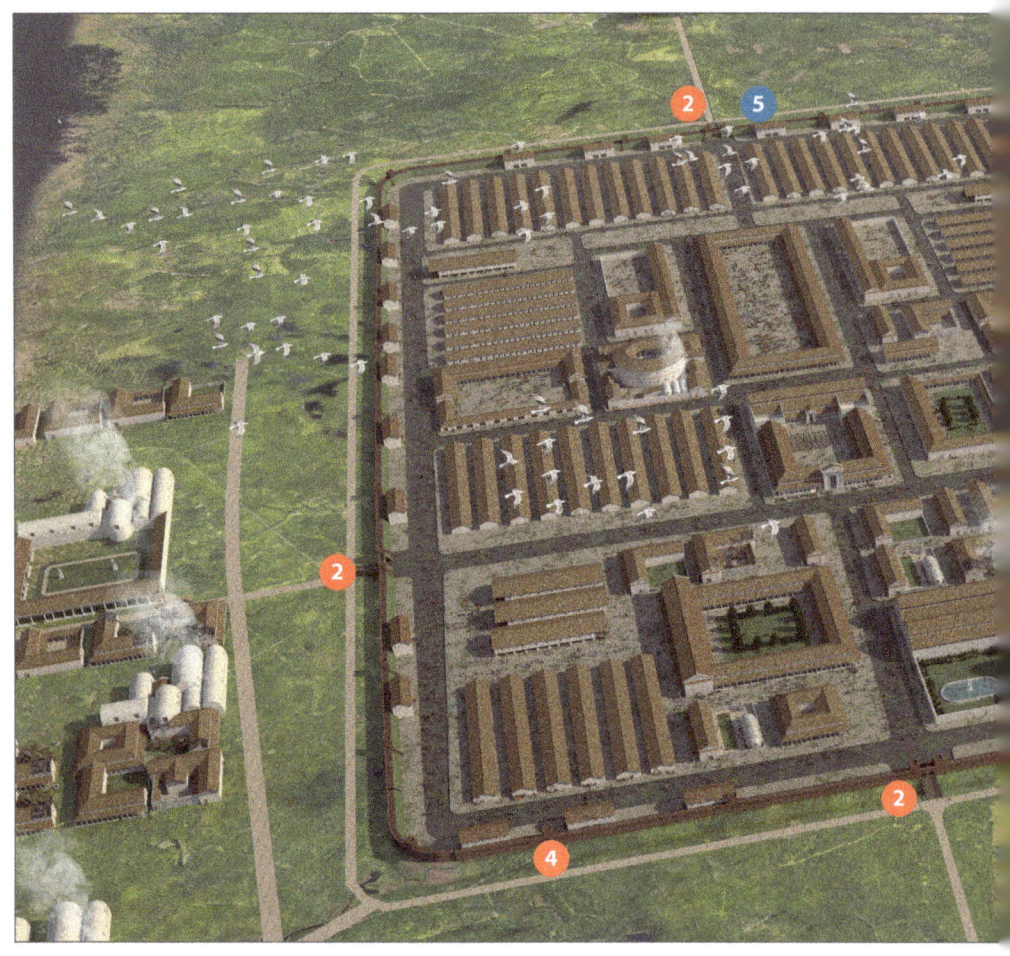

The Fortress Wall, looking north, in 276 CE.

The Fortress Wall

One of the first tasks of building the Roman fortress was to build its defences. This would have involved digging out ditches surrounding the fortress to stop it being overrun, and soil would have been used to add height to a wooden defensive wall. There were also towers along the wall with gatehouses at key points. Around 100 CE the wooden fortress wall was replaced with a red stone wall. It would have been around 6 metres *(20 feet)* high and surrounded the whole perimeter of the fortress. The Roman Wall was built in a much more complex way than most other Roman fortresses, possibly due to Chester being the intended centre of Roman Britain and Ireland *(see page 10)*. There were also four gatehouses which allowed entry into the fortress as well as 22 towers including the South-East Angle Tower *(see page 16)*. A small section of the wall can be seen to the east of Northgate, by the canal.

Key

- Roman Walls[1]
- **1** Eastgate
- **2** Gatehouse
- **3** South-East Angle Tower
- **4** Tower
- **5** Roman Wall

1. Note that most of Chester's city walls are post-Roman and only partially follow the line of the Roman walls. (See page 32 for more details).

CGI model based on archaeological data produced by Dr David Mason FSA MCIfA

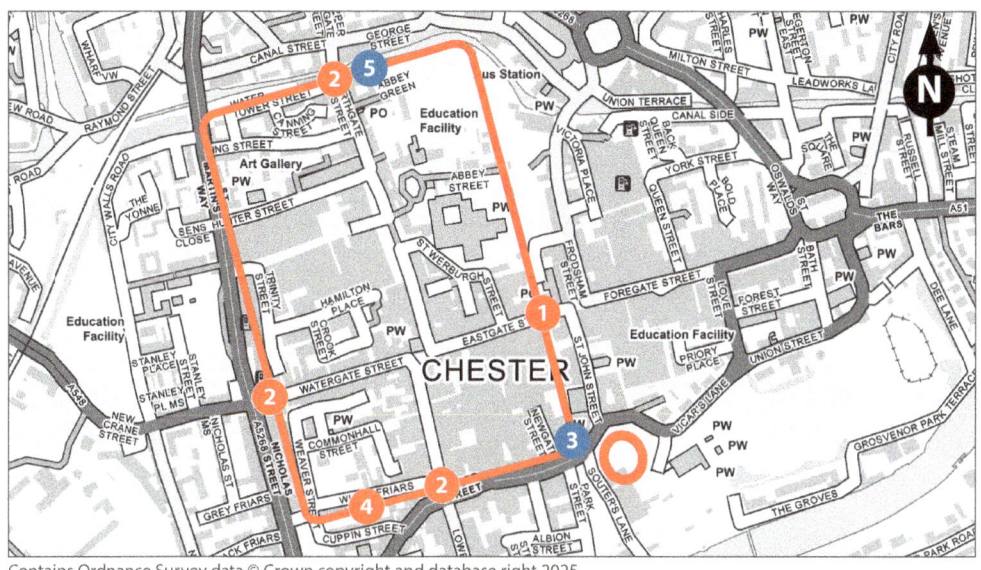

Contains Ordnance Survey data © Crown copyright and database right 2025

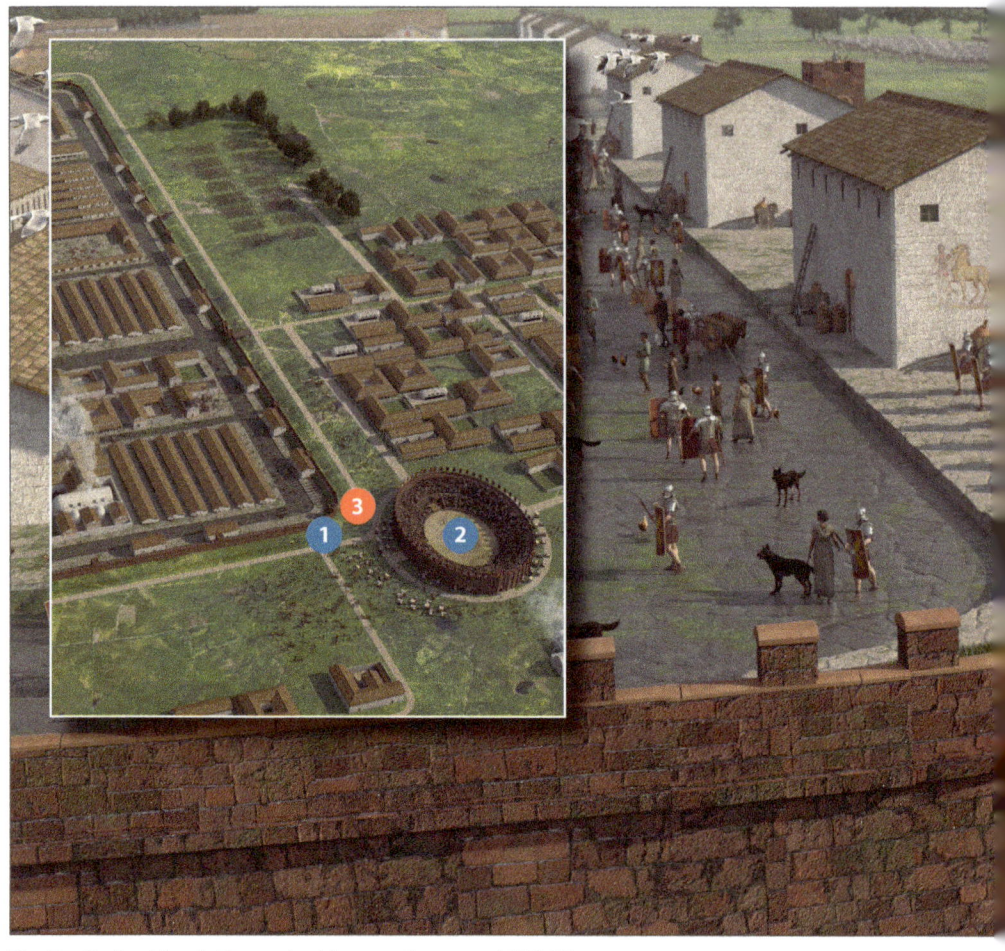

The South-East Angle Tower, looking north, around 276 CE.

The South-East Angle Tower

This tower was built at the same time as the rest of the Fortress wall *(see previous page)*, and its foundations can still be seen, next to the remains of the amphitheatre. The wall, gatehouses, towers and ditch defences[1] would have made the fortress extremely difficult to attack. *Ballistae*[2] may have been placed on all of the corner towers to defend the fortress. There were only three[3] legionary fortresses in Roman Britain: Caerleon, York and Chester, which was the largest of the three.

1. The ditches were 2.7 metres (9 feet) deep and 6 metres (20 feet) wide.
2. Ballistae were huge crossbows that by the 4th century could fire stone balls or metal bolts.
3. Other fortresses included Colchester and Lincoln, but these became colonia, the rough equivalent of cities.

Key

— Roman Walls[4]
1. South-East Angle Tower
2. Amphitheatre
3. Defensive ditch

4. The main illustration shows the complex construction of the wall including intricate wall mouldings.

CGI model based on archaeological data produced by Dr David Mason FSA MCIfA

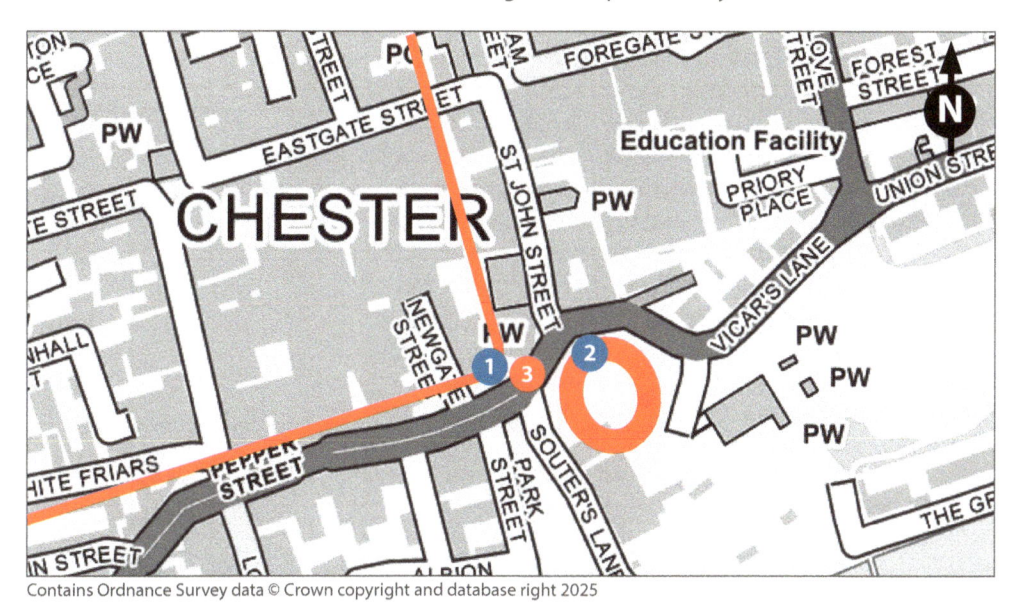

Contains Ordnance Survey data © Crown copyright and database right 2025

The site of the Elliptical Building, looking north, 276 CE.

The Elliptical Building

In 1939 a very unusual building was uncovered in Chester, which has puzzled archaeologists ever since. What it was built for has led to many theories including a market, theatre or part of a palace. The current view seems to be that it was possibly a highly elaborate market hall. The Elliptical Building is thought to have been part of the original design of the fortress and was started around 78 CE. But the building was abandoned along with the rest of the fortress *(see page 8)* and was used as a rubbish dump and storage area.
Building work on the Elliptical Building, and the rest of the fortress resumed around 230 CE, although it was built to a slightly different plan from the original. The 15m *(49 feet)* construction also had other connected buildings including its own bathhouse. This building and the large storage building, next to it, all point to the Romans at one point having great plans for Roman Chester *(see page 10)*.

Key
— Roman Walls
1. Elliptical Building
2. Bathhouse
3. Bathhouse columns[1]
4. Large store building

> 1. Columns from the Elliptical Building's Bathhouse can be seen in the Roman Gardens, which are a modern arrangement of Roman artefacts.

CGI model based on archaeological data produced by Dr David Mason FSA MCIfA

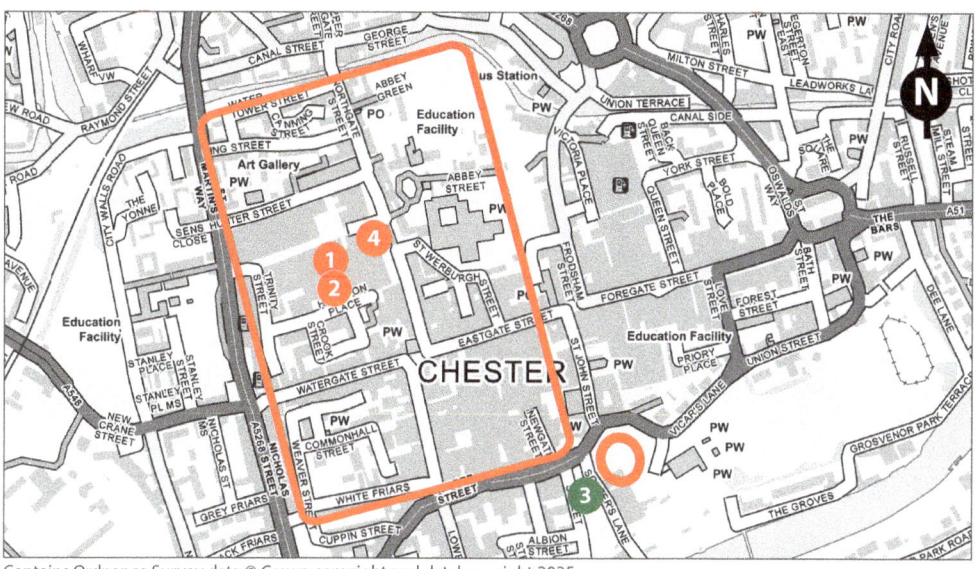

The site of the Principia, looking north, 276 CE.

The Principia

The *Principia*[1] was the centre of the fortress where the Legionary standards[2] were kept. It also acted as the administrative hub of the fortress, such as the logistics needed to keep the fortress maintained and everyone fed. The *Principia* also had a heavily protected strongroom, where the legion's money was kept. Most Roman fortresses had two main roads, the *Via Principalis (loosely translated as 'way to the Principia')* and the *Via Praetoria (loosely translated as 'the way to the Praetorium')*. The *Legatus Legionis (a rough equivalent of a general)* typically occupied the *Praetorium (shown on the main image, next to the Principia)*. Here matters such as how the army would be deployed were discussed.

1. The Principia was probably built around 78 CE.
2. Standards were symbols carried into battle on tall poles, which partly represented the legion and the power of Rome.

Key

— Roman Walls
1. Principia
2. Praetorium
3. Principia Strongroom[3]
4. Principia column[4]

3. There is a dedicated display showing a small section of the Principia strongroom, on Hamilton Place (see online for details).

4. Column visible in 21-23 Northgate Street.

CGI model based on archaeological data produced by Dr David Mason FSA MCIfA

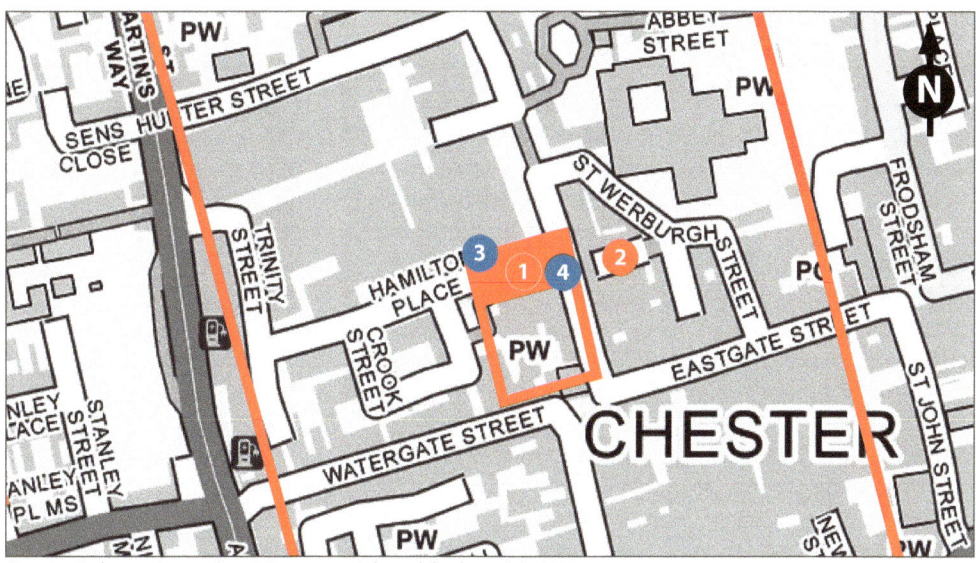

Contains Ordnance Survey data © Crown copyright and database right 2025

A speculative view of the Fortress Bathhouse, looking north, 276 CE.

The Fortress Bathhouse

On the south side of the fortress was a large military bathhouse, which would have had a furnace to heat the *Caldarium (hot room)* and the *Tepidarium (warm room)*. There was also a *Frigidarium (cold room)*, and a large *Palaestra (exercise area)*. The soldiers would have bathed and socialised, in some ways like in our present day swimming pools. Personal hygiene was also seen to be important for the soldiers' health. The Romans did not have soap products, so instead used oil and scraped the oil off with a curved implement called a *strigil*.[1] The bathhouse may have had many other facilities such as an *Apodyterium (heated changing rooms)* and possibly a library. Other bathhouses have been found, including a public one connected with the Elliptical Building *(see page 18)*.

1. *A strigil and other Roman bathing items can be seen at the Grosvenor Museum.*

Key

— Roman Walls
1. Fortress Bathhouse[2]
2. Warm room
3. Cold room
4. Exercise area
5. Public Bathhouse
6. Principia
7. Parade ground

2. *A small section of the Bathhouse can be seen in the basement of the Bridge Street Café.*

CGI model based on archaeological data produced by Dr David Mason FSA MCIfA

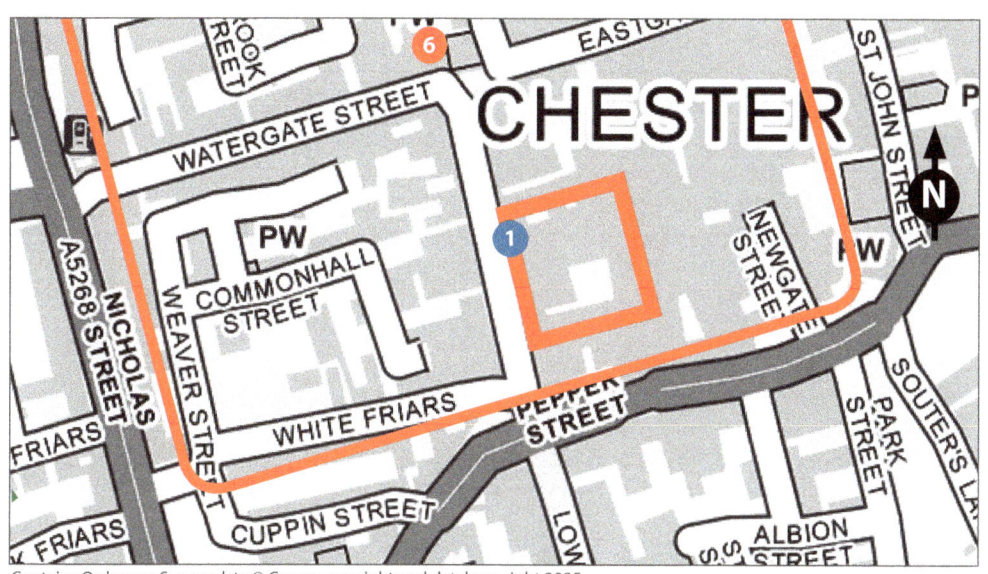

Contains Ordnance Survey data © Crown copyright and database right 2025

A view of the Roman Port, looking north, 276 CE.

The Roman Port

At first glance, it may seem strange that the Romans had a port serving Roman Chester, but the course of the River Dee was very different in Roman times[1]. This would have allowed Roman ships to connect with the Irish Sea and the rest of the Roman Empire. There was a jetty where boats could unload cargo. On the edge of the racecourse is a section of the quay[2] where boats could also offload their cargo.[3] After the Roman period, the River Dee began to silt up, so that ships started to offload their cargo in Liverpool. In the 18th century the river was diverted with a canal *(marked with black arrow on map)*.

1. For example, the area where Chester racecourse is now located was then underwater.
2. Some think it is a section of the fortress, rather than the quay.
3. Amphorae which were used to transport foods from the Mediterranean can be seen in the Grosvenor Museum.

Key

— Roman Walls
1. Roman Port
2. Quayside
3. Warehouse
4. Jetty
5. Roman Ship
6. Trireme (Roman warship)
7. Public Bathhouse

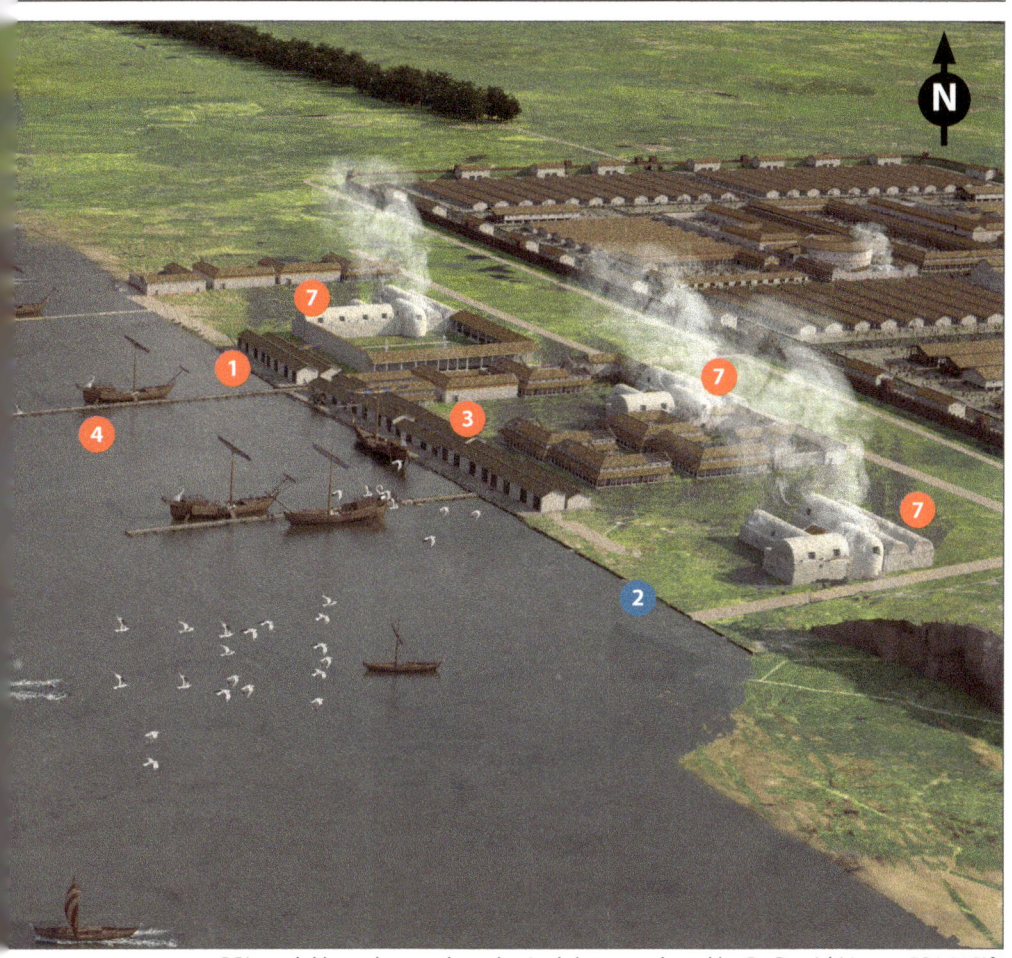

CGI model based on archaeological data produced by Dr David Mason FSA MCIfA

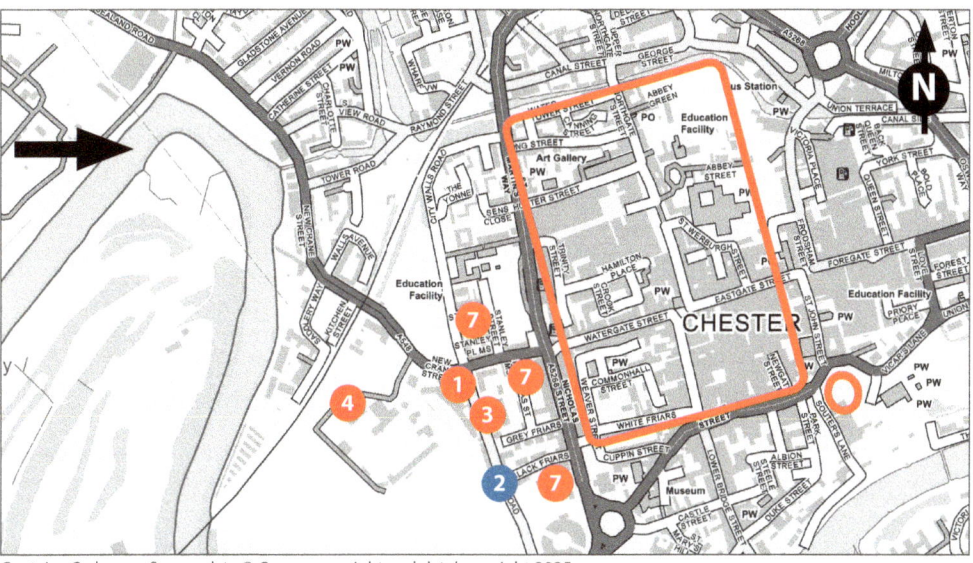

Contains Ordnance Survey data © Crown copyright and database right 2025

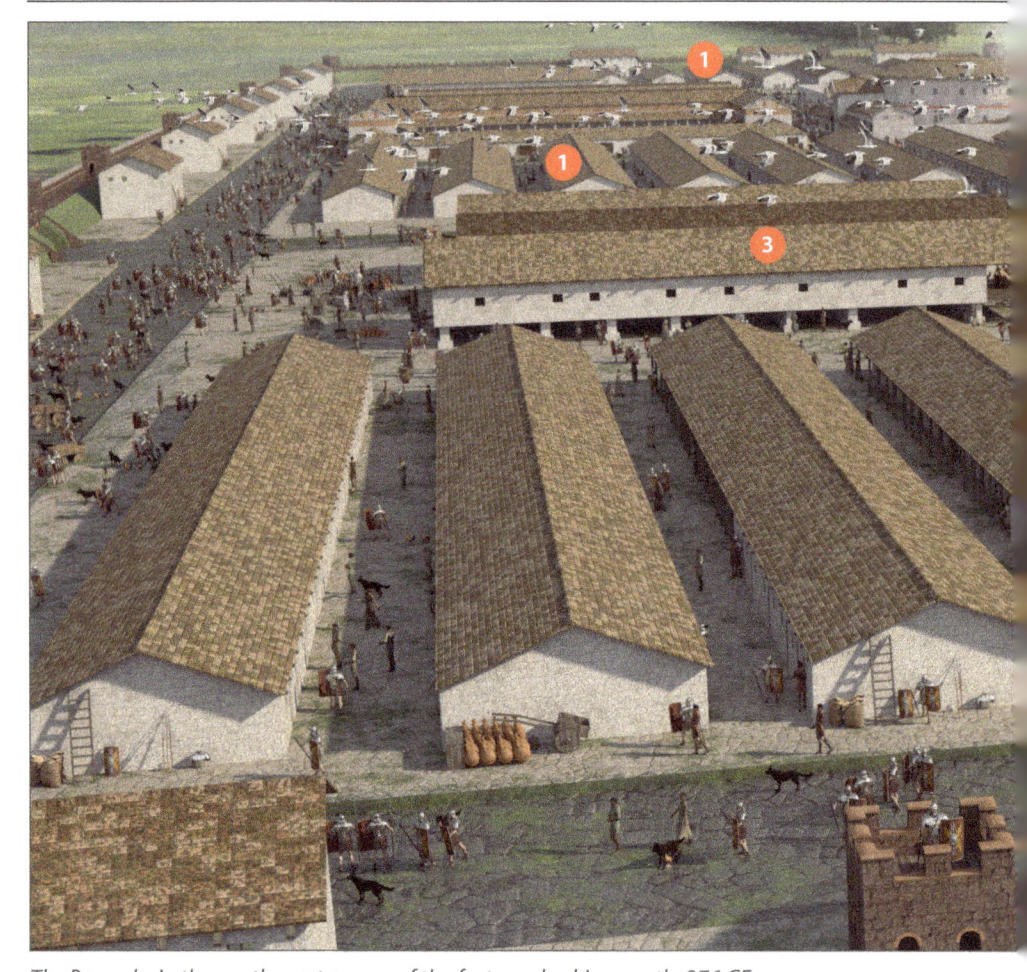

The Barracks in the south-west corner of the fortress, looking north, 276 CE.

The Barracks

The soldiers based at Chester[1] all needed accommodation which was called a *Praetentura (Barrack)*. A barrack housed a *Legionary century (made up of eighty Legionaries and a Centurion)*. Each barrack was probably split into two sections, one for commanding officers such as the *Centurion* and one for the eighty *Legionaries*. The *Centurion* would have had space appropriate to his rank, including an office to keep each *century* running properly. This involved logistics and discipline. There was far less space for the *Legionaries* who were split into groups of eight, each with two rooms, one for them and one for their equipment. Spare rooms were used to accommodate new recruits or other soldiers.

1. These were first from the Legio II Legio II Adiutrix (Second Legion Helper) and later from the Legio XX Valeria Victrix (Twentieth Victorious Valeria Legion). See page 30 for more details.

Key

— Roman Walls
1 Barracks[2]
2 Boar Sculpture[3]
3 Granary
4 Hospital

2. There are models of the barracks and military artefacts inside the Grosvenor Museum (yellow square).
3. Outside the front of Chester market is a modern sculpture of a boar, which was the symbol of the Legio XX Valeria Victrix.

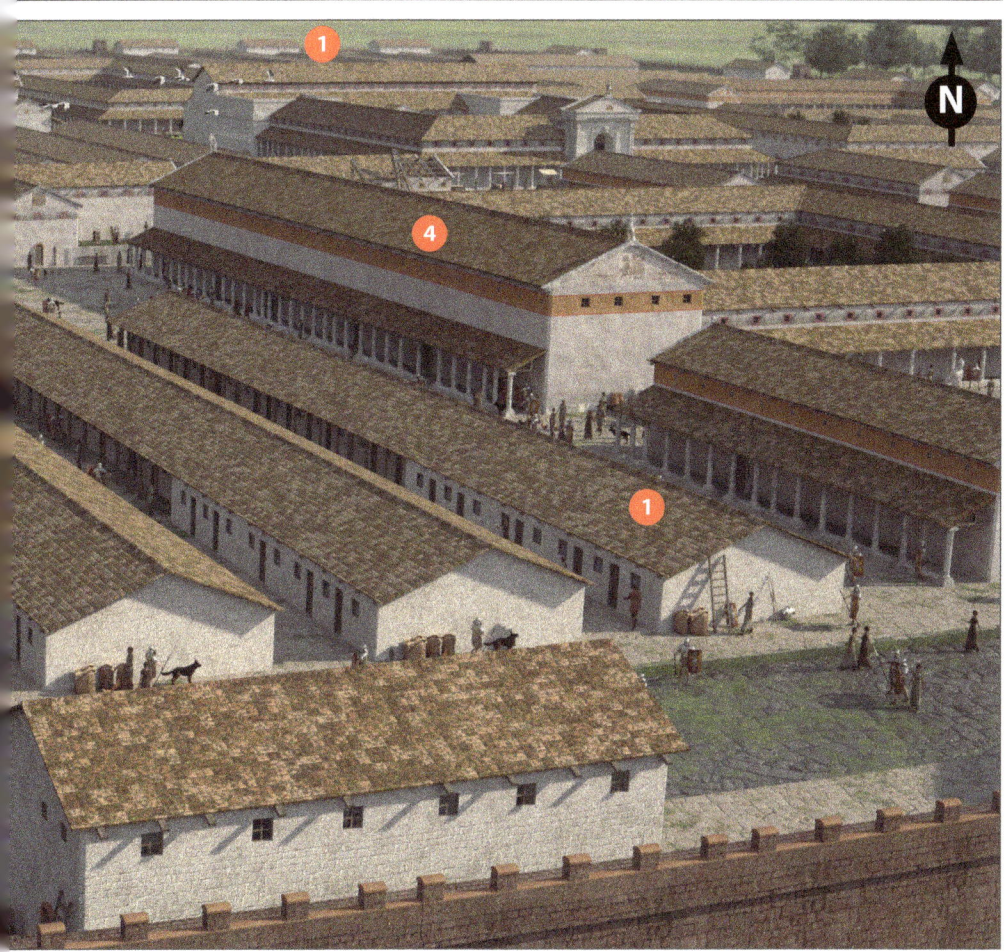

CGI model based on archaeological data produced by Dr David Mason FSA MCIfA

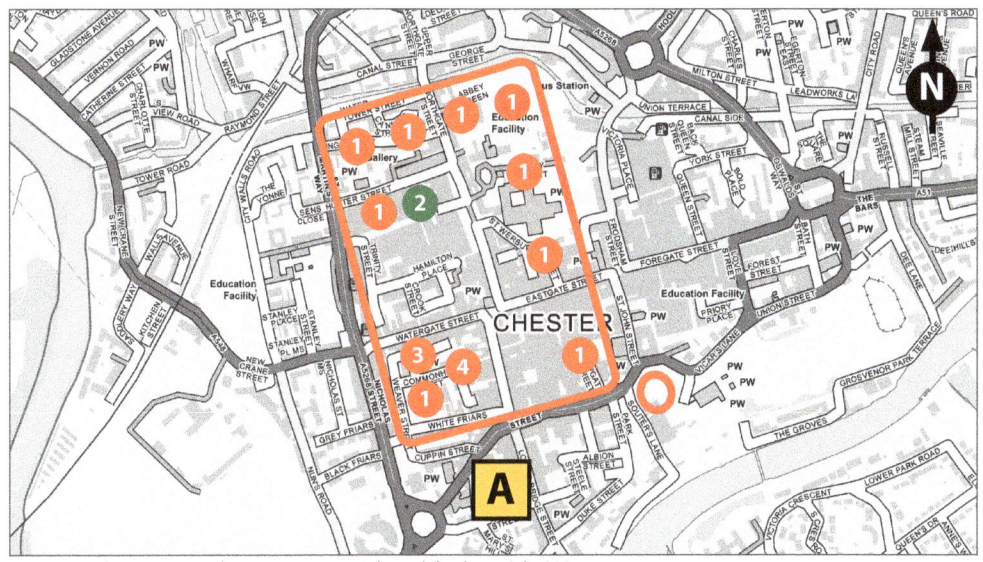

CHESTER

A

Contains Ordnance Survey data © Crown copyright and database right 2025

A view of the Hospital, looking north, 276 CE.

The Hospital

The Romans did not have many hospitals, although they could be found in military bases such as the one at Chester. The Roman expansion of the empire of course did not come without cost, with many soldiers injured during their years of service. The Romans believed that the Gods caused illness and thought that prayer and rituals would help alleviate suffering. As the Roman Empire evolved, and with influence from the Greeks, medical practice changed, with more practical approaches. The *Medicus (Doctor)* was one of the highest ranking members of the fortress.

The *Valetudinarium (hospital)*[1] was used to help treat the fortress soldiers with a mixture of basic *(compared to modern times)* medical practice and religion. Treatments included extensive use of herbs such as sage and fennel.

1. Army hospitals were often able to treat up to 500 soldiers at one time, in wards, like modern hospitals.

Key

— Roman Walls
1. Hospital
2. Medical stores
3. Surgeries
4. Isolation area
5. Religious area
6. Principia
7. Elliptical Building

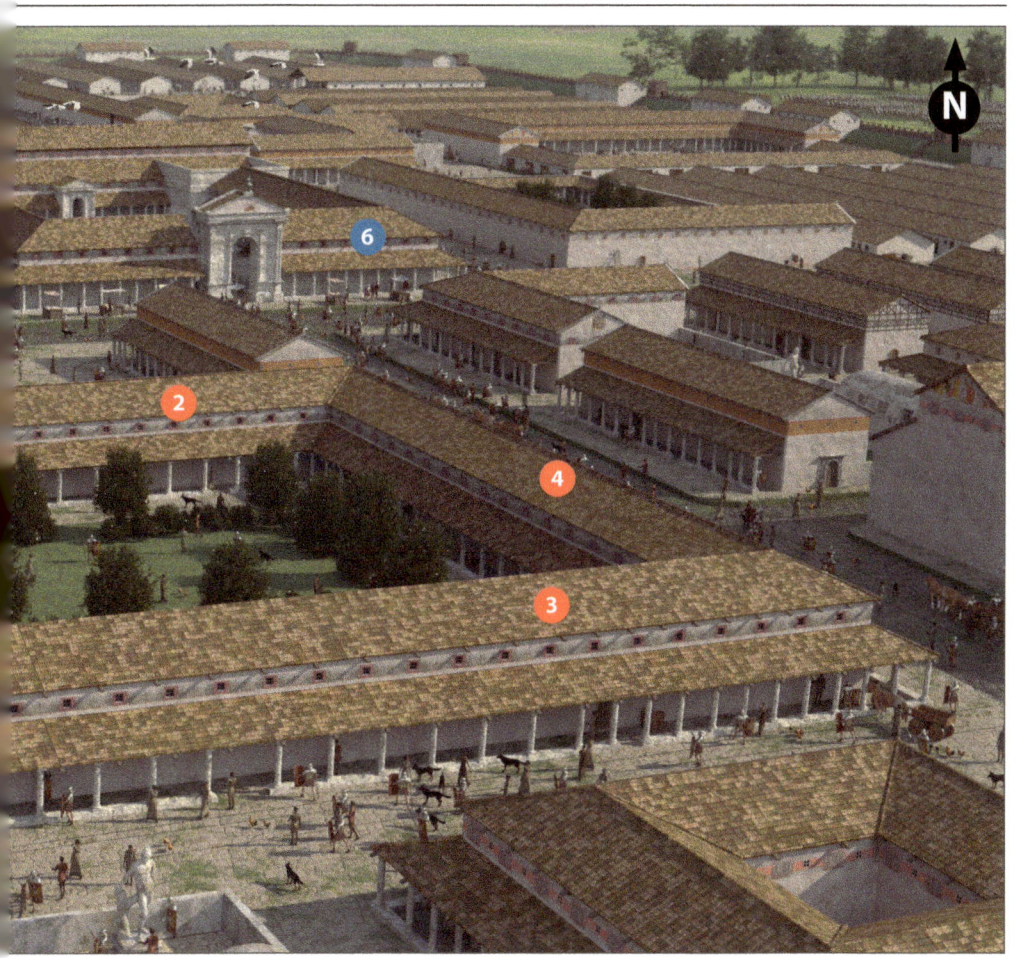

CGI model based on archaeological data produced by Dr David Mason FSA MCIfA

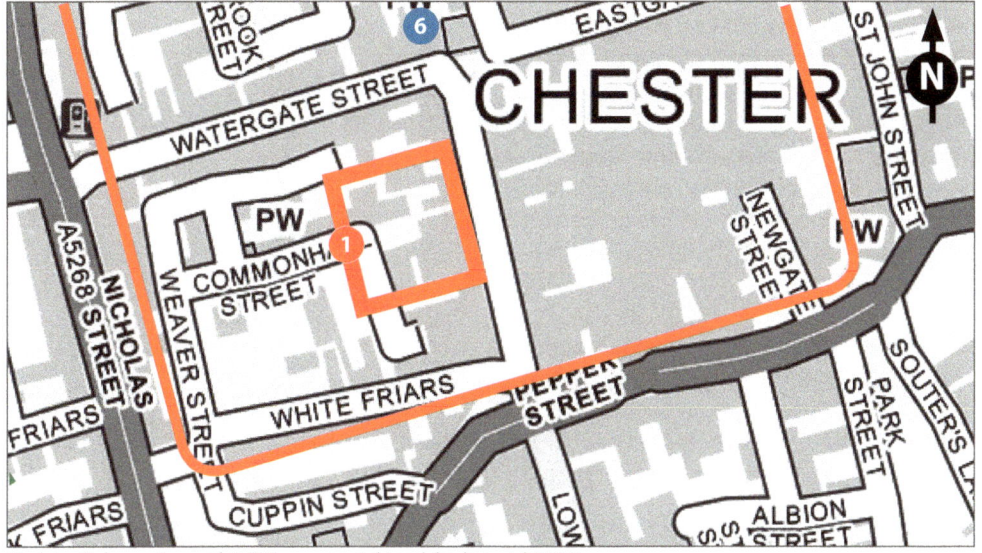

Contains Ordnance Survey data © Crown copyright and database right 2025

A view showing typical weapons and equipment used by the Twentieth Legion.

The Twentieth Legion

The *Legio XX Valeria Victrix (Twentieth Victorious Valeria Legion)*, which upgraded the fortress at Chester[1], was one of the original four legions which invaded Britain in 43 CE. The map on the right shows how much they were moved across Britain, starting with the invasion of Colchester, then moving west to fight the *Silures* in South Wales. They were deployed to defeat *Boudica*[2] at Watling Street, near St Albans, before going to North Wales to fight the Druids. Later they were sent to southern Scotland before moving to Chester. Each legion had a symbol associated with it, the Twentieth Legion's symbol was the boar[3].

1. The fortress was established by the Second Legion.
2. Boudica and 120,000 warriors burnt Colchester to the ground.
3. A metal boar can be seen outside Chester market (see page 26), and a Roman artefact with the boar symbol can be seen in the Grosvenor Museum.

Key

1. Pilum (Javelin)
2. Scutum (Shield)
3. Focale (Scarf)
4. Gladius (Sword)
5. Galea (Helmet)
6. Lorica Segmentata (Body Armour)[4]
7. Tunica (Tunic)
8. Caligae (Sandals)[4]

4. Examples of these items can be seen in the Grosvenor Museum.

A possible route used by the Twentieth Legion from 43 CE to 88 CE

- **A** *Richborough*
- **B** *Colchester*
- **C** *Usk*
- **D** *Watling Street*
- **E** *Anglesey*
- **F** *Wroxeter*
- **G** *Inchtuthill*
- **H** *Chester*

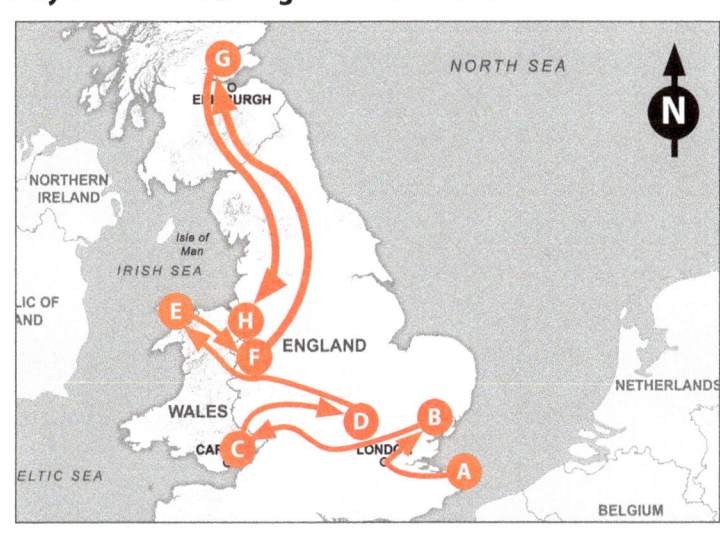

Contains Ordnance Survey data © Crown copyright and database right 2025

32. Roman Chester today

Roman Chester today

Chester has a long and rich history and today is a thriving city. It can be difficult to interpret what is Roman and what is post-Roman, especially with the city walls. Most of the city walls visible today date from after the Roman period.
The sites shown on this map are explored in more detail in the main part of this book, as well as showing where the main museums in Chester are that feature Roman artefacts. Also indicated are modern recreations of Roman sites and artefacts, such as the Roman Gardens.
All the illustrations of Roman Chester face north.
Map based on archaeological data produced by Dr David Mason FSA MCIfA

Key

- **1** *Roman site, which has visible remains*
- **2** *Roman site, which has no visible remains*
- — *Roman wall, which has no visible remains*
- — *Post-Roman wall*
- **A** *Museum, which has visible Roman artefacts/remains*
- **11** *Recreated Roman site or artefact*

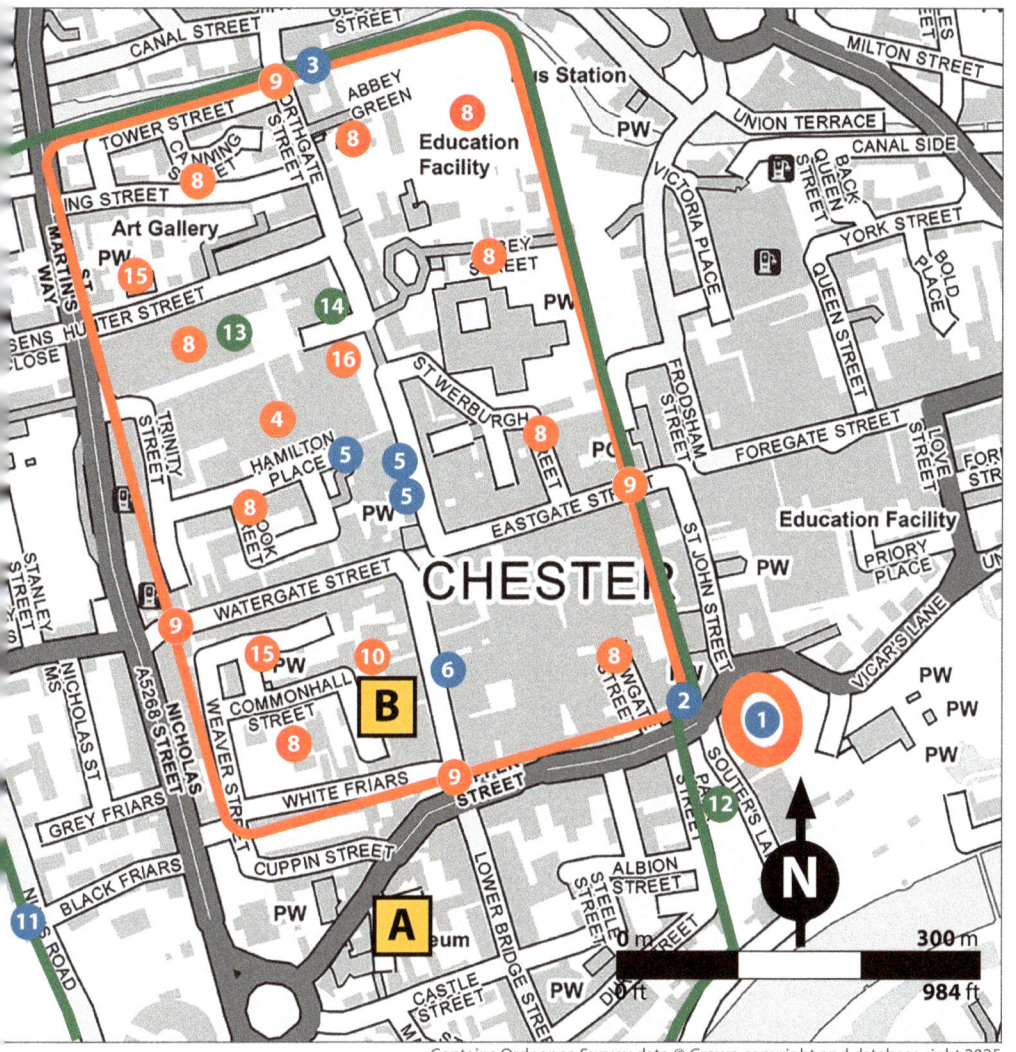

Contains Ordnance Survey data © Crown copyright and database right 2025

--- Fortress Wall (p. 14)
1. Amphitheatre (p. 12)
2. S.E. Angle Tower (p. 16)
3. Fortress Wall (p. 14)
4. Elliptical Building (p.18)
5. Principia (p. 20)
6. Fortress Bathhouse (p. 22)
7. Roman Port/Jetty (p. 24)
8. Roman Barracks (p. 26)
9. Roman Gatehouse (p. 14)
10. Roman Hospital (p. 28)
11. Roman Quay? (p. 24)
12. Roman Gardens (p.18)
13. Roman Boar (p. 26)
14. Roman Columns (p.18)
15. Roman Granary (p. 26)
16. Storage building (p. 18)

A *The Grosvenor Museum. The museum has extensive displays, artefacts and mosaics from the Roman period, including artefacts from the Roman Army (p.30).*

B *Deva Roman Experience. The museum recreates what life was like in Roman Chester.*

JC3DVIS
CONCEPT DESIGN

First published June 2025
ISBN 9781068352515 *(Paperback)*
First Edition

Designed and published by JC3DVIS
www.jc3dvis.co.uk
Book design © 2025 Joseph Chittenden

All the images in this guide were produced by JC3DVIS.
Contains Ordnance Survey data © Crown copyright and database right 2025

The moral right of the copyright holder has been asserted.

All rights reserved. No part of this publication may be reproduced, distributed or transmitted in any form or by any means, including photocopying, recording, or other electronic or mechanical methods, without the prior written permission of the publisher.

With special thanks to:
Dr David Mason FSA MCIfA
Jane Chittenden *(Research, writing and proofreading)*

Legal disclaimer
Neither the author nor the publisher shall be held liable or responsible to any person or entity with respect to any loss or incidental or consequential damages caused, or alleged to have been caused, directly or indirectly, by the information contained herein.

Bibliography and sources

- De la Bédoyère. Guy: *Roman Britain, A new history*
- Mason. David: *Excavations at Chester*
- Goldsworthy. Adrian: *The Complete Roman Army*
- https://researchframeworks.org/nwrf/roman-resource-assessment-2007/
- https://www.cheshirewestandchester.gov.uk/documents/planning-and-building-consultancy/total-environment/PRDG/2.3-Brief-history-of-Chester-1.0.pdf
- https://chesterwalls.info/gallery/oldmaps/index.html *(shows River Dee before canal)*
- Roman_Chester_2065135893 *(PDF download by Chester VIC, accessed online)*
- https://www.british-history.ac.uk/vch/ches/vol5/pt1/pp1-8#n6
- https://historicengland.org.uk/services-skills/education/educational-images/roman-shrine-to-minerva-chester-6675
- https://www.romanroads.org/gazetteer/cheshire/cheshire.html
- Visit to the Grosvenor Museum, Chester

www.ingramcontent.com/pod-product-compliance
Lightning Source LLC
LaVergne TN
LVHW060747090725
815724LV00020B/727